Tesseract

poems by

Kimberly G. Jackson

Finishing Line Press
Georgetown, Kentucky

Tesseract

Copyright © 2016 by Kimberly G. Jackson
ISBN 978-1-944251-48-2   First Edition
All rights reserved under International and Pan-American Copyright Conventions. No part of this book may be reproduced in any manner whatsoever without written permission from the publisher, except in the case of brief quotations embodied in critical articles and reviews.

ACKNOWLEDGMENTS

Grateful acknowledgment is made to the editors of the journals in which the following poems first appeared:

Boston Poetry Magazine: "Eulogy"
Kind Over Matter: "Last Words"
Literal Latté: "August Midnight, 1996"
Millennium New Writings: "For a Posting of Banns"
Möbius: A Journal of Social Change: "Bedtime on Independence Day"
Wild Violet: "The Frozen Alster," "Kaddish for Mr. Rosenbaum," and "Tesseract"
Words Dance Publishing: "The Women of the Ruins" (in an earlier version)
Writer's Digest: "Brushing My Daughter's Hair"

Editor: Christen Kincaid

Cover Art: Kimberly G. Jackson

Author Photo: Kimberly G. Jackson

Cover Design: Elizabeth Maines

Printed in the USA on acid-free paper.
Order online: www.finishinglinepress.com
Also available on amazon.com

Author inquiries and mail orders:
Finishing Line Press
P. O. Box 1626
Georgetown, Kentucky 40324
U. S. A.

Table of Contents

Wayne H. (1947-1988) 1

August Midnight, 1996 3

The Women of the Ruins 4

Baby Wash, October 23, 1962 7

Kaddish for Mr. Rosenbaum 8

Mojave Memory, 1974 11

Tesseract: A Parent's Guide to Time Travel 13

For A Posting of Banns 15

The Frozen Alster 16

Last Words 17

Bedtime on Independence Day 18

Since 1943 19

Visions of Naia 20

Eulogy 21

Brushing My Daughter's Hair 22

Audiophile 23

American Saints 25

For Mark

Wayne H. (1947-1988)

I'm cross-addicted! he'd announce
Almost as if celebrating
Anonymity be damned.
He painted it on his pickup
Above a skull and bones

He was barrel-chested then
A talker, fast and loud
I'd answer my father's phone, "Richman Roofing,"
And he'd bellow down the line:
*Thisis**PART**ofRichmanRoofing!*
So glad to be alive and with us
Able to hammer for hours in the sun
Haul shingles up a ladder on his back
Stay for late-night poker
Fueled by coffee and cream soda

In the rooms he'd say *I'm Wayne*
And when they said *Hi Wayne* he'd tell them
About guns and needles
Prison and a virus
But much more
About how good it was now

He had time to find a wife
She was funny, freckled, kind
To go once with my parents to Vegas
The only other time I left the state I was in custody! he laughed
And to bring coffee cake and chat with the newcomers

The night he died my father sat beside him
I'll tell them, Wayne said, *to save a seat for you
at the big poker table in the sky*

That week, the people stood to ask
For courage and for wisdom in his name
There were three coffee cakes, plus ice cream
And the Saturday game went all the way till dawn

August Midnight, 1996
(141 East 13th St., New York City)

In 4A, a thin young woman
Checks the lock the stove the lock
Lies down, gets up to do it all again
Twenty, thirty times before she rests
Shallow sleep of caffeinated brain
Muscles not unfurled
Coiled, as they will be decades later
When she strokes her daughter's hair at bedtime
Swearing silently she will not check downstairs

The women in 4B are drinking, lasciviously
As is their wont.
Gin washing vodka washing champagne washing skin
Bass rippling from their stereo through the walls
My God I love you says the older one through laughter
As if she'll never regret it
And she won't
Even when her tawny beauty's gone

And upstairs the English teacher
Who does not yet know that she has cancer
Is breathing in the smell
Of a man who thinks she's funny
Who will marry her in a dance hall
And who, on the morning the Towers fall, will weep
Not for them but for her, sitting beside him in frozen traffic
When she should be getting chemo
Waiting, dying slowly on a bridge

Above their roof the harvest moon grows dim
Outshone by the city's lambent globe
And the traffic pulses red-white-red through spacetime
Every flash a heart, a mind, a soul

The Women of the Ruins

Berlin, 1946

Zoom in above the bombed-out city
Watch the figures in the rubble breathe to life
Start the soundtrack: *scritch-a-scritch a-*
as they grab the bricks and with their brushes
scritch-a-scritch
reclaim them for the nation one by one
See a small girl sorting gravel, sharp and gray
It looks just like her eyes
This is my mother, before I was.

Hastings, 1976

Take a close-up of the kitchen light
shaking as the crashing peaks
Pan out to see my mother in short shorts
carrot in her hand
broken chair backs, severed table legs around her
My father's naked chest is glazed with sweat
Are you happy now, he asks her
are you happy are you now
her face is blank
the carrot crackles like a fire in her teeth.

Later that night:

Scan my canopy bed where
Daddy's belly spoons my back
His fingers smell like pickles
and his lips like smoke
I can hold my breath
but I can't stop my heart
thrumm thrumm thrumm thrumming in my head

By day she's always driving
I watch and wonder if she's real
or is the skin I love to smell
stretched across a robot's mask
My hands and head float huge
above the bedtime sheets she tucks
swelled by questions I can't ask
as her nails click off the light

Providence, 1990

Her eyes stay on the road.
Those are lies you learned in therapy
it's those lesbians at school
after all he's done for you
let me give you some advice

Brooklyn, 2003

My husband, my husband, I say to keep me here
but every pad of his fingers corkscrews through my flesh
swift tunnels bored through muscle fat and skin
Feet breast cunt mouth ass hand neck tongue
all shoot separate sparks
that burn and blind and soon there is no one
to whom it happens
It is only happening
I'm gone.

Lake Mohave and Niagara Falls, 2011

His obituary's short and rimmed in black
He's gone, now, after all you put us through
she writes me, staring at the lake at lowest ebb
Twenty feet of bleached white rock exposed

Wind blows through me like an X-ray
I stand seared to bone
Cue the noise of freight cars rushing on the track
See me call to my own children
pull them in before the rain
and hide my tears like secrets in their hair

See us locked in double freeze-frame
And before the pixels move

FADE TO BLACK

Baby Wash, October 23, 1962
For Jeanne

While Cuba waited
My mother-in-law wept
Into the washing machine

She thought her three boys
Might never grow
To be anyone's husbands

If those men with missiles
Exchanged swelling clouds of ash
Across the seas

All the bedtimes naptimes mealtimes
Lullabies purées and games
Would vanish in a single flash

But if those idiots don't do it
She thought, I'll need clean diapers
So she did what women do

Mix your tears with soap and bleach
Turn the dial to extra hot
Press go

Kaddish for Mr. Rosenbaum

Yitgadal v'yitkadash sh'mei raba

I am Rivka, a convert, bat Avraham ve Sarah
also daughter of Christa, whose first memories are of craters made
by English bombs in Hamburg streets
granddaughter of Lotte, who died in Marburg
the day the Wall came down
adopted niece of Hilde, Lotte's childhood friend
who decades later became my own.

b'alma di v'ra khir'utei, v'yamlikh malkhutei

Lotte, my Oma, came to New York every summer
Bringing strange toothpaste and lotion and chocolates I loved
Speaking to my mother a language I didn't understand
And telling me stories, always the same ones, of her husband, her
children, and Mr. Rosenbaum.

b'hayeikhon u-v'yomeikhon u-v'hayei dkhol beit yisrael,

"He was our teacher in the high school, and all the girls loved him,
he was so kind
He took us on class trips, and we would sing: he had a beautiful voice.
He would lead us through the fields, singing.
All of us loved Mr. Rosenbaum."

ba'agala u-viz-man kariv
v'imru amen.

Always, over and over the same,
The schoolgirl's affection still shining from her
at fifty-five, sixty and seventy-one
So that I came, with teenage wisdom, to say yes, Oma, we know

We know all about Mr. Rosenbaum

Y'hei sh'mei raba m'varakh l'alam u'l'almei 'almaya.

She never talked about the war.
Except to say terrible, terrible I pray never again

Yitbarakh v'yishtabah v'yitpa'ar

Years later I ask Hilde, I want to know
She says terrible, terrible, but we didn't know any Jews
v'yitromam v'yitnasei
How could we know?
V'yit-hadar
It happened early in the mornings
v'yit' aleh v'yit-halal
We didn't know any Jews
sh'mei d'kudsha
We didn't know, I didn't know
b'rikh hu

Last year my mother told me.
"They knew people who were killed, of course they did.
Tante Paula, your great-grandmother's cousin: she married a Jew.
One night they both disappeared. She came back alone, later, and
they'd ransacked her apartment—
There was nothing but trash in empty rooms.
Kaftanski was his name."

l'ela min kol birkhata v'shirata, tushb'hata

And you know, the teacher, Mr. Rosenbaum.
He was a Jew. One day they went to school
and all the Jewish teachers were gone."

*v'nehemata da-amiran b'alma
v'imru amen.*

She never told the end of the story.
She only spoke of songs and fields.

Y'hei sh'lama raba min sh'maya

I don't know his Yahrzeit.
I don't know his place of death.
I don't know his first name.

v'hayim aleinu v'al kol yisrael

I know all the girls loved him
I know he was kind
I know he used to sing
He had a beautiful voice

v'imru amen.

This is not a poem
It is not a "poem after"
It is Kaddish
Only Kaddish

Oseh shalom bi-m'romav, hu ya-aseh shalom

I will not forget
I will not forget

*aleinu v'al kol yisrael
v'imru amein.*

Mojave Memory, 1974

Mom and Dad and the little girl I was
Got out to look
Out over a vast red meteor crater

Except it can't have been one of the famous ones
Because we were alone
No cars up and down the two-lane blacktop
Splashed with silvery puddles of mirage

Space swooped open, wide beneath our feet
Empty sky expanded overhead
But what I remember most was how it sounded:
A silence so big it roared in our ears

It's what you hear if you subtract
Not only traffic, and voices
But crickets, and birdsong
Rustling of leaves river rain
A nothing that is hugely something
And that held us, vibrating, in the winter sun

Now I have a daughter, and I think:
What were they thinking?
Miles from any town, or even gas station
For sure without enough water
Or knowledge of auto repair
Cell phones not even dreamt of

But then I see their youth
Mom's green-checked sundress
Dad's slim black jeans
Their child, in pigtails

And knowing all that was lost later
I touch again that moment
When we stood, all three, so still
And felt the warm fullness at the center of the world

Tesseract: A Parent's Guide to Time Travel
With thanks to Madeleine L'Engle

A tesseract, you may recall, acts like a wrinkle in time
Cinching together *now* and *long ago* or
Right this minute and *decades hence*
Like a pleat, a hem
Or a cloth swept from the table
All whorls and fluting, rapidly compressed.

It's what they nowadays would call a wormhole
And say you need a warp drive to approach.
But parents generate them just by being:
Seed them with our breath
Spark them with our glance
Roil spacetime's fabric with our every step.

You know it from yourself:

How the smell of chlorine can transport you
To those mornings with your mother at the pool
Her laughter at the cold and splash and rush of it
Your buoyancy, and hers

How maraschino cherries take you back
To the diner where your father met his pals
His smoky smell, the crinkles round his eyes
And how you craved their light.

So we outlive ourselves
Our images self-assembling
In a son or daughter's view
Bright holograms that hearten, soothe, or sear.

It's something, you might say, to bear in mind:

That this little girl
Who takes forever to put her shoes on
Who will never, ever, go to sleep
Will one day be waiting at a stoplight
Or pause while paying a bill
And zoom back along the timeline to today.

When you look at her, see that woman
A little tired, maybe tense
With the lines of age just starting near her mouth
Watch her face change as she's struck
By a sudden memory of you
Exactly as you are right here and now
Meet her gaze
And make her smile at the thought.

For a Posting of Banns

What occurs, you know, occurs so slowly. At first it's blossoms on windowsills, plums sugar-tart, silk-satin brushing skin. Not bad at all, I admit. It's only gradually that a worry starts. And it is only that. Not anguish—not mostly, anyway, although at particular instants, that may roar forth, volcanic—but say, for now, just worry. As if from a raspy throat/aching back/minor virus. Small things of that kind. Plus, you do find a bit of conflict: not too much, mind you, just a flash now and again—which, you think, is hardly unusual. It stings, but just for an hour. And a dulling—both of touch and of insight—is obviously normal. Only natural. In fact, a common topic. So you go on. In daily traffic that is always flowing, branching, looping through a country that grows awfully familiar. You may not crash; you may hit no major disruptions. But bit by bit, you'll start to switch things out. As if transforming a vast wall brick by brick, so that nothing falls, but nothing stays. Or moving a highway inch by inch until it points north, not south. Pick your own damn analogy. My point is that without any outward sign, your rock, your compass, your guiding light, will shift; what was most rapturously crucial to your soul will vanish from it. And what's worst about it is how smoothly it will go, without your noticing what's missing. How you will not think to cry, or stop to mourn what's lost.

The Frozen Alster

Hamburg wraps itself around two lakes
Formed by the river Alster.
Once in a very rare winter they freeze solid
Conjuring new space in the center of town.
A sudden shortcut in the sunshine
A huge white loop to skate or ski
A nighttime fairground where you go to drink hot *Gluehwein*
Bought from lantern-lit booths suspended over water.
To eat sweet powdered pastries and hear accordions play
To watch the crowds of people laughing
On a street that's made of waves.

It's something to see but I never saw it
Twenty years ago, at twenty-three.
My bus stopped right around the corner at the *Rathaus*
Every day I wanted to go look
But grief had cut the circuit
Connecting wish to act
Had shrunken movement to a shuttling
On a single tunneled track.
I knew it lay just out of sight, beyond the building's edge
Where brindled stones, tight-mortared, mounted to the sky.
A viscid nausea coiled around my ribs
Want but can't want but can't want but can't
Until there was no longer any choice.

You could say it's the reason
I saw Christo wrap the Park
Why I walked the Golden Gate despite the wind
And I greet the ocean every summer day I can.
But it's also why I sometimes dream
Of winter dryads locked in leafless wood
Their heartglow ebbing almost to the root
Arm-branches outstretched, black and stiff with ice.

Last Words

*Every two weeks, one of the world's languages is lost
as its final native speaker dies.
(Factsheet, Living Tongues Institute for Endangered Languages)*

She sings herself a song. Her mother knew
it, and her son, long gone
It tells of birds that fly on
silvered feathers to the moon

Bedtime on Independence Day
(After Emma Lazarus)

In the summer of 2014, thousands of unaccompanied minors crossed Mexico's border with the United States.

The GOP congressman says we should not give
the impression they can stay. *The coyote left me*
says Angel, 13, *and I walked alone in the desert.* *Your
policies did it,* the president's enemies say. *They're tired
and hungry and scared,* says the priest. *They spend your
tax dollars,* says the radio man. *Their homes are poor
and murderous,* says the advocate. *Stay close to your
brother* were Ana's grandmother's last words. *Huddled
in detention centers,* the newswoman says, *these masses
are overwhelming. I don't fault their yearning*
says the mayor, *but.* I stop reading to put my kids to
sleep. Their great-grandparents came in steerage. It hurts to breathe
as I watch their faces: drowsy, safe and free

Since 1943

Berlin's saved a spire
Stark amid the bustling shops
A ghost who saw fierce
Flags and boots march tattered home
To rooms opened to the sky

DC's not haunted
By what burns in ancient sands
Melts in tropic green
Hides draped in wood, unpictured
Or dreams of drowning in light

Visions of Naia

The Bering-strait theory of human migration to the Americas has been strengthened by an analysis of remains found in a flooded cave in the Yucatán Peninsula. While divers could not raise the entire skeleton of the teenaged girl—nicknamed Naia by scientists for the water nymphs of legend—-they extracted a single tooth, which yielded DNA proving links both to Asiatic peoples and to modern Native Americans. Researchers theorize that the girl died in a fall after entering the cave in search of a drink, one hot afternoon more than 12,000 years ago.
New York Times, 5/15/2014

Pain sears through dank air
Rocks slick-sharp on knees
Fear cold wet seeping
Hair floats on black sea

Outside men shouting
Red torches, no rest
A woman rocks, stares
At the fire blindly

The centrifuge tears
Secrets from proteins
Fingers tap keyboards
While a vast family

In cars schools parks stores
Breathes, vibrant, blooming

Eulogy

I felt my father's death in aisle six
His favorite ice cream stared me in the eye
He's gone, the freezer whispered, you can't fix
The pain between you. It's too late to try
He isn't eating thickly buttered toast
Or watching Mets play baseball on TV
Not reading headlines in the *New York Post*
Not cursed or blessed by any thoughts of me.
His socks and gloves and belt are empty, left
His hammer's still, his nails, his roofing truck
And I, his child, estranged, heartsore, bereft
Remember him and wonder how the fuck
It's possible that he does not exist:
This man so deeply feared, and loved, and missed.

Brushing My Daughter's Hair

Recessive genes surprised us with her flaxen helixed curls;
Fifty microns leaves a world of room to tangle. When she's forty,
Will she still know I finger-combed to gentle out the knots?

Audiophile
For Michelle

It's a gut renovation or teardown
No one who can afford waterfront
I watch my wife. Sun glares

Through her childhood bedroom
Like neon tracing white vellum
Lines around her eyes

I'll take the bleeding hearts
She whispers in our bed
And the slate stones

From inside, I want the sounds—
Audio keepsakes. Houses, it seems
Have timbres, keys, riffs

She used to fall asleep listening
To her mother's shower
Busy day washing warm away

Wake to the breakfast-rattle stovetop
Wait for her tread on the stair
Click of the doorknob she touched

People are taken, or go
In flashes of blood anger smoke
Or slowly, as passages close

What's left is the lowing
Of windows in storm
Creak-ache of wood glass and iron

Till these too are silenced
And only their ghosts
Roam through fresh sheetrock pipe tile

Can she transmute solace
Into pulses on circuits
And hold memory in the palm of her hand?

She doesn't wake
As I curl myself to her
And listen as if for an answer

But I hear only her breathing
And my heart in my ears
And outside, unceasing, the rain

American Saints
(With thanks to Neil Gaiman)

Among those removed from the list of official saints in 1969 were Catherine of Alexandria, legendary scholar, orator, and patron of female students; and Christopher, the longtime protector of travelers and bachelors. Catherine's feast-day, November 25th, was restored to the Roman calendar as an optional celebration in 2004.

From <u>Hagiography Post-Vatican II</u>

Opening the oven to check the pies, she remembers the Summer of Love. The strawberries he bought her with his last dollar, the long aimless walks along the waterfront. Sometimes she misses that tiny apartment where they lay curled together in the glow of the streetlamp, sleeping through the traffic that rumbled behind the curtains like rain. Once he started working at the docks she spent so many nights alone, grading papers at this kitchen table. Still she smiles, shelling the peas, to recall how his crew loved him. Trusted him with their lives, told him all their troubles. Of course she treasured those nights too, the ones spent reading and writing to her more-than-children, the girls who passed through her hands each year, opening like flowers to her voice. Nothing's changed, she realizes, as she moves to the sink, even now that he's at the airport: those young kids in their TSA uniforms hang on his every word, and he works all the late shifts while she writes, sometimes till dawn. The Old Man, they call him, and they say he sees everything. So strange that he's *her* old man—she who swore, long ago in her desert city, that she'd never marry. She thought no male could ever tolerate her reason—not, of course, that he always could. The corners of her eyes crinkle as she sees again the nights he's lain, rough-hewn features turned from her, his dark bulk breathing, silent. Would it have been different, she wonders on her way to the hall cupboard, if they'd had a son he could carry on his shoulders? Certainly, but there's really no telling if better, or worse. In the end we both did what we were meant to do, she thinks, marveling at his shoes next to hers on the doormat, his jacket touching arms with her coat. She unfurls the red tablecloth, watches it billow, fall. Looks up to see him huge in the doorway, watching her, his blue eyes shining. We have a choice, she tells herself. Let's set a feast.

Notes

"Baby Wash" uses the triversen poetic form; "Since 1943" uses the tanka; "Visions of Naia" is a bref double; "Last Words" is a Welsh englyn; "Eulogy" is an English sonnet; "Brushing My Daughter's Hair" is a sijo; "Bedtime on Independence Day" uses the golden shovel form, in which the final words of each line, read in order, form a line from another poem; and "For a Posting of Banns" is a lipogram which does not use the letter "e."

Additional Acknowledgments

Thanks are due to Robert Lee Brewer, whose prompts on his Poetic Asides blog at Writer's Digest Magazine provided inspiration for many of these poems, and to the many writers and readers who make that blog community such a supportive one for new poets.

I am also grateful to Michelle Lamb for proofreading, and to everyone at Finishing Line Press for their help and support.

Finally, warmest thanks to Mark Evan Chimsky—my kind first reader, gentle editor, and dear friend.

Tesseract is Kimberly G. Jackson's first chapbook. Her poems and flash fiction have appeared in a number of literary journals, including the *Boston Poetry Magazine, Corium, Kind over Matter, Literal Latté, Möbius: A Journal of Social Change, New Millennium Writings, Spillway, Wild Violet,* and *Words Dance Publishing*. She has also been nominated for the Pushcart Prize. Kimberly lives in Newton, Massachusetts.

Her website is http://www.tesseractpoet.com.

www.ingramcontent.com/pod-product-compliance
Lightning Source LLC
Chambersburg PA
CBHW051705040426
42446CB00009B/1319